Ready, Set, Write!

A Student Writer's Handbook

for School and Home

By the Editors of TIME FOR KIDS

Ready, Set, Write!

TIME FOR KIDS® BOOKS
Editorial Director: Keith Garton
Design Production: Georgia Rucker
Project Editor & Design:
The Quarasan Group, Inc.

Teacher Editorial Board:
Holly Albrecht, WI; Marian Evans, TX;
Judy Holtmyer, OK; Ryann Kelso, IL;
Karen Lawson, OH; Christine Libeu, CA;
Karen Mauro, NY; Julie Morgan, NE;
Mary Paskvan, MN; Jeff Reed, PA; Jana
Underwood, TX

TIME INC. HOME ENTERTAINMENT
Publisher: Richard Fraiman
Executive Director, Marketing Servies:
Carol Pittard
Director, Retail & Special Sales: Tom Mifsud
Marketing Director, Branded Businesses:
Swati Rao
Director, New Product Development:
Peter Harper
Financial Director: Steven Sandonato
Assistant General Counsel: Dasha Smith Dwin
Prepress Manager: Emily Rabin
Book Production Manager: Jonathan Polsky
Marketing Manager: Kristin Treadway
Retail Manager: Bozena Bannett
Special Sales Manager: Ilene Schreider
Associate Prepress Manager:
Anne-Michelle Gallero
Associate Marketing Manager:
Danielle Radano

Special Thanks:
Alexandra Bliss, Glenn Buonocore, Patrick
Dugan, Suzanne Janso, Robert Marasco,
Ed Matros, Brooke McGuire, Chavaughn
Raines, Adriana Tierno, Britney Williams

TIME For Kids and the Red Border Design
are registered trademarks of Time Inc. For
information on TIME For Kids magazine for the
classroom or home, go to
www.timeforkids.com and look for "Subscribe"
or call 1-800-777-8600.

Copyright © 2006

ISBN: 1-933405-38-4

Published by TIME For Kids Books
Time Inc., 1271 Avenue of the Americas
New York, New York 10020

Send your comments and suggestions
about TIME For Kids Books to info@
timeforkids.com or write to: TIME For Kids
Books, Attention: Book Editors, PO Box
11016, Des Moines, IA 50336

Photography credits:
Page 5: PhotoDisc, Inc.; p. 6: Comstock; p. 8: PhotoDisc, Inc., MetaTools; p. 9: MetaTools; p. 10:
MetaTools; p. 11: MetaTools; p. 12: MetaTools; p. 14: PhotoDisc, Inc., MetaCreations/Kai, Corbis; p. 16:
PhotoDisc, Inc.; p. 18: PhotoDisc, Inc.; p. 20: PhotoDisc, Inc.; p. 24: PhotoDisc, Inc., MetaCreations/
Kai; p. 31: PhotoDisc, Inc.; p. 33: PhotoDisc, Inc.; p. 34: PhotoDisc, Inc.; p. 36: PhotoDisc, Inc.; p. 37:
MetaCreations/Kai; p. 38: Comstock; p. 40: MetaCreations/Kai; p. 41: Wildside Press; p. 42: PhotoDisc,
Inc.; p. 43: PhotoDisc, Inc.; p. 46: MetaCreations/Kai, PhotoDisc, Inc.; p. 47: PhotoDisc, Inc.; p. 51:
PhotoDisc, Inc.; p. 54: PhotoDisc, Inc.; p. 60: Artville; p. 62: Corbis; p. 69: PhotoDisc, Inc., Artville; p. 73:
MetaCreations/Kai; p. 80: MetaCreations/Kai, PhotoDisc, Inc.; p. 81: PhotoDisc, Inc.; p. 82: PhotoDisc,
Inc.; p. 83: PhotoDisc, Inc.; p. 84: PhotoDisc, Inc.

 For more writing practice: www.timeforkids.com/hh/writeideas

Table of Contents

Using Your Writer's Handbook

Do you know the secret to becoming a better writer? Write, and then write some more!

At TIME For Kids magazine, writers go through many of the same challenges that you do as you write. The TFK writers must find a topic, research the facts, get organized, write a draft, revise their writing, and edit and proofread their writing. Think of writing as a process, steps that can help you become a better writer.

Your TIME For Kids Writer's Handbook is a handy tool you can use when you write. In your Handbook you will find:

- a guide to the writing process, featuring a section about each of the steps that good writers follow.
- mini-lessons on skills such as writing smooth sentences.
- samples of different kinds of writing you'll have to do at school, from reports to poetry.
- places to record words that will make your writing clear and interesting.

Remember, have fun with your writing. Find an idea or story that matters to you and makes you want to write. Ready, set, write!

Time to Write: The Writing Process

Steps in the Writing Process

1 Prewriting—Choose a topic. Then plan and organize what you are going to write about.

Jake, my pet snake

green
shiny black eyes

sticky tongue
likes to flick

2 Drafting—Write your ideas down in a rough draft, or first copy.

I have a pet snake named jake.

He is green and has shiny black eyes.

He also has a sticky tonge. Jake likes

to flick his tongue

3 Revising—Get other readers' responses through sharing and reflecting. Make changes to improve your draft.

Meet Jake

I have a pet snake named jake.

He is emerald green and has shiny

black eyes. He also has a long sticky

tonge. Jake flicks his tongue to catch

food to eat

4 Editing and Proofreading— Find and fix any mistakes.

Meet Jake

I have a pet snake named jake.

He is emerald green and has shiny

black eyes. He also has a long sticky

tongue
~~tonge~~. Jake flicks his tongue to catch

food to eat

5 Publishing—Write your final copy and share it with others.

Meet Jake
I have a pet snake named Jake. He is emerald green and has shiny black eyes. He also has long sticky tongue. Jake flicks his tongue to catch food to eat.

TFK Tips for Writers

You can go back and repeat a step any time during the writing process.

Now let's take a closer look at each step in the writing process.

Prewriting

Prewriting is the time to plan and organize what you are going to write about. One way to do this is to draw a picture of the topic you have chosen and then list words that describe it.

Jake, my pet snake

green

shiny black eyes

sticky tongue

likes to flick tongue

Drafting

Drafting is the time to get your ideas down on paper. Use your notes from the Prewriting activity to write your first draft. Don't worry about mistakes. You can fix those later.

I have a pet snake named jake.

He is green and has shiny black eyes.

He also has a sticky tonge. Jake likes

to flick his tongue

Revising

Revising is the time to think about your writing and share it with others. Get responses from other readers. Use their comments and your own ideas to make changes that will improve your draft. What changes did the writer make to improve the draft on page 9?

Meet Jake

I have a pet snake named jake.

He is emerald green and has shiny

black eyes. He also has a long

sticky tonge. Jake flicks his tongue

to catch food to eat

Editing and Proofreading

Editing and Proofreading is the time to find and fix any mistakes before you make a final copy. Notice how the writer used proofreading marks to show what needed to be fixed.

Meet Jake

I have a pet snake named jake.

He is emerald green and has shiny

black eyes. He also has a long

tongue
sticky ~~tonge.~~ Jake flicks his tongue

to catch food to eat

Publishing

Publishing is the time to write your final copy and share it with others.

Meet Jake

I have a pet snake named Jake. He is emerald green and has shiny black eyes. He also has a long sticky tongue. Jake flicks his tongue to catch food to eat.

Prewriting

Time to plan and organize what you are going to write about

Getting Started

Where do writers get ideas? Writers get ideas from the world around them. They write about people they know, places they visit, things they do, and topics that interest them.

Look and Listen!

Writers look and listen. They notice things such as colors, sounds, and smells. Look at these pages from a writer's notebook. How did the writer describe her surroundings?

Smelled in Springtime

rain

orange blossoms

Try This!

Start your own personal writer's notebook. Keep it with you so that you can write anywhere and anytime. Then be aware. Make notes in your notebook about things you see and hear. Warm up by adding to each entry in the writer's notebook below.

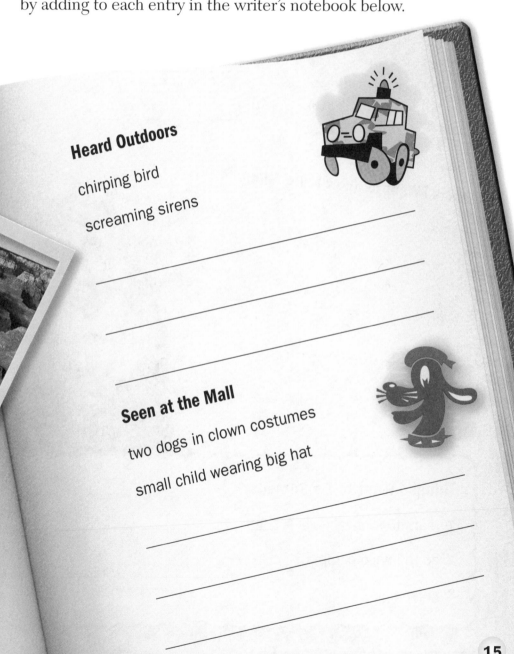

Heard Outdoors

chirping bird

screaming sirens

_____

_____

_____

Seen at the Mall

two dogs in clown costumes

small child wearing big hat

_____

_____

_____

Be a List Keeper

Good writers are list keepers, too. Making lists gives them ideas for topics to write about. You can keep your lists in your writer's notebook. How would you complete each list on this page?

Fun Places I Have Visited

1 Wisconsin Dells

2 Disney World

3 Grand Canyon

4 _____

5 _____

Animals I Want to Know More About

1 hamsters

2 lions

3 _____

4 _____

5 _____

Things I Want to Do Someday

1 learn to swim

2 go to space camp

3 go camping

4 _____

5 _____

Try This!

Here are some more lists. How would you complete each? Write your ideas.

Favorite Games

1 basketball

2 hopscotch

3 soccer

4 _____

5 _____

Top Ten Fun and Fun-to-Say Words

1 tiny

2 swish

3 fussy

4 crash

5 cheese

6 _____

7 _____

8 _____

9 _____

10 _____

Time to Write

Make your own list. Write a title for the list. Then review your list when you need to find a topic to write about.

Title: _____

1 _____   **4** _____

2 _____   **5** _____

3 _____   **6** _____

Choose a Topic

As part of Prewriting, you need to choose a topic to write about. That's when your writer's notebook comes in handy. You can review your notes and choose an idea that would make a good topic.

Narrow It Down

When you write, make sure your topic is not too big. Choose an idea that you can write about easily in one piece of writing. If your topic is too big, you may need to narrow it down, or break it into smaller parts. You can use an idea comb to help you.

Idea Comb

my pet frog Frodo

| how to take care of a pet frog | why a frog makes a good pet | the time Frodo escaped |

TFK Tips for Writers

Talk about your topic ideas with a partner. Which ideas does your partner like best?

Some topics are too big to write about—there is just too much to say. Using a topic map like the one below is another way to narrow your topic. It will help you choose an idea that you can write about in a story or brief report.

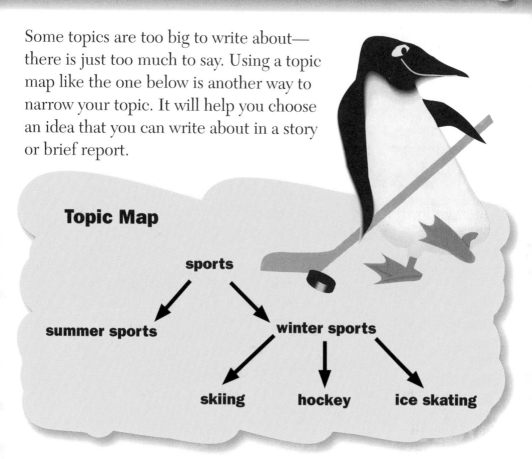

Topic Map

sports

summer sports

winter sports

skiing

hockey

ice skating

Try This!

Look at a topic you are planning to write about. Is it too big? Use one of the organizers shown here to narrow it down. On a separate sheet of paper, write your big idea. Then write smaller parts of that idea below. Choose one small part to write about.

TFK Tips for Writers

When you get ready to write, choose a topic you can write about easily in one piece of writing.

Start Thinking

You've chosen a topic and narrowed it down. Now think about what you want to say and how you will say it. The questions below can help you.

Ask Before You Write	
What am I writing?	Am I writing a fable or a folktale? a report? a letter?
Who is my audience?	Is it my teacher? my classmates? my parents?
What is my purpose?	Do I want to entertain? to inform or explain? to persuade someone to do something?
Do I have all the facts I need?	If not, where can I look? Will I use an encyclopedia or atlas? Internet sites or nonfiction books?
How will I publish my writing?	Will I publish it on a school Internet site or make a book? Will I read it in class or give a speech? Will I include photographs or illustrations?

Try This!

What are you planning to say about your topic? How are you planning to say it? Before you begin, ask yourself the questions in the chart. Use your answers to help you plan what you want to write.

Organize Your Ideas

Once you have decided what to write about, you need to arrange your ideas in a way that makes sense.

Use a Graphic Organizer

You can use graphic organizers to help you organize your ideas. Here are two examples. You'll find many others on TIME For Kids Homework Helper site: **www.timeforkids.com/hh/writeideas**

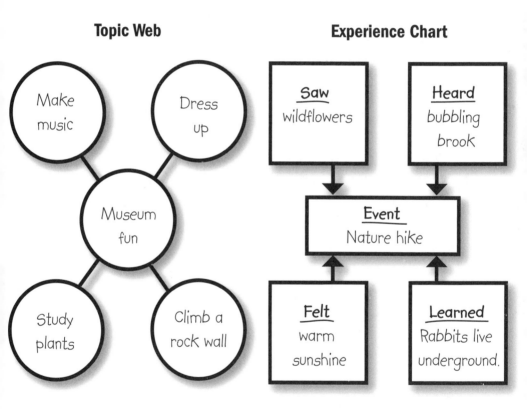

Topic Web

Make music

Dress up

Museum fun

Study plants

Climb a rock wall

Experience Chart

Saw
wildflowers

Heard
bubbling brook

Event
Nature hike

Felt
warm sunshine

Learned
Rabbits live underground.

Use a topic web to plan a report, an article, or a biography. An experience chart works well for planning a personal narrative.

More Graphic Organizers

Fiction Story Map	
Beginning	On a rainy morning, Meg is surprised when a gust of wind carries her into the sky.
Middle	Meg has several adventures visiting places around the world, such as the Great Wall of China and the Eiffel Tower, as she tries to make her way home.
Ending	Almost ready to give up on ever seeing her home and family again, a magical seagull carries Meg home.

Use a fiction story map to plan a fable, folktale, fantasy, or adventure story.

Try This!

Here is a Venn diagram you could use to plan a paper comparing dogs and cats. When you write to compare, you tell what is different and what is the same about each person, animal, or object. How would you complete the diagram?

Dogs

bark

gnaw on bones

_____

Both

have fur

need food

_____

Cats

meow

climb trees

_____

2

Drafting

Time to write
a working draft,
or first copy

What Is a First Draft?

A first draft is your first attempt to write something. It is your chance to get all your ideas down on paper.

Tips From a Pro

Read the interview with writer Cindy Crown below. What tips does she give to help you write a first draft?

Interview with a Writer

Q. When you begin to write, what do you do first?

A. First, I think about my ideas and make a plan. I think about what I want to say and how I want to say it. I also think about whom I'm writing for.

Q. What do you do next?

A. Next, I just start to write. I write down all my ideas. I don't worry if my writing doesn't sound right. I write on every other line of my paper so that it's easy to make changes later.

Q. If you are not sure about how to spell a word, what do you do?

A. I usually circle the word. The circle reminds me to check it later in a dictionary.

Q. Why is it important to write a first draft?

A. A first draft gives me a chance to get down all my ideas without having to stop. Then I can check a dictionary or think about the order of my ideas.

A Sample First Draft

Read the excerpt shown below. It is from a first draft of a story about a make-believe character. What did the writer do to show that he or she is not finished writing this part of the story? Do you see other changes that the writer might make?

MeMe

MeMe

There are many chores that I have to do, but there is one chore that I don't have to do anymore. Guess who has to do that chore now. My (imajineree) friend does it!

Does this belong here?

Her name is MeMe. She is half cat and half horse, and she has wings. MeMe is two years old. So, she can take me to (skool) and she will pick me up to go home. I love to ride MeMe everywhere.

What Is Fiction?

Fiction is a kind of writing that has made up characters and events. Narrative fiction includes folktales, fairy tales, fables, fantasy, and stories about people like you.

Folktales and Fairy Tales

Folktales and **fairy tales** are fiction. These kinds of stories often include pretend characters such as elves and animals that can talk. Folk and fairy tales often begin "Once upon a time." *Stone Soup* is a folktale. *Hansel and Gretel* is a fairy tale.

Try This!

What folktale or fairy tale do you know? Write the title below. What makes it a folk or fairy tale?

_____

Fables

Fables are fiction. Fables are stories that teach a lesson or moral. They may also have animal characters. The *Tortoise and the Hare* is a fable. So is *The Grasshopper and the Ant*.

Try This!

What fable do you know? Write the title below.
What makes it a fable?

_____

Fantasy

Fantasy stories are fiction. Fantasy stories often have magical characters. They may also take place in magical places where anything can happen. *Alice in Wonderland* is a fantasy.

Try This!

What fantasy story do you know? Write the title below.
What makes it a fantasy?

_____

TFK Tips for Fiction Writers

- Use your imagination.
- Tell the story in order.
- Draw pictures.

Time to Write

Look at a fiction story you are writing. Read the tips in the chart. Which tip could you try?

Story Pieces

A story is like a puzzle. It has pieces that fit together to make a story picture. The pieces, or parts, of a story are characters, setting, and plot.

Parts of a Story

- The **characters** are whom the story is about.

- The **setting** is where and when the story takes place.

- The **plot** is what happens in the story. It tells the problem that the characters have and how they solve it.

TFK Tips for Writers

Use an organizer like the Fiction Story Map on page 22 to plan and draft your story. Be sure to write the events in the order they happened.

Time to Write

Look at a story you are writing. Does it tell who the characters are and what the setting is? Does it tell what the characters' problem is and how they solve it? If not, add the missing story pieces.

Creating Characters

Good writers use details to describe story characters. The chart below shows details that can help make characters seem real.

Character Details

- **How a character looks** Is the character a person, an animal, or a fanciful elf or giant? Does he or she have horns or pink hair? wear green, pointed shoes or an oversized red sweater?

- **How the character acts or feels** Is the character silly? curious? shy?

- **What the character does or likes to do** Does the character like to help people? Does he or she fly? travel back in time?

TFK Tips for Writers

Including dialogue, the speakers' exact words, can bring your characters to life.

Time to Write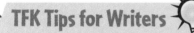

Look at a character from a story you are writing. Add details to describe the character more clearly and make the character seem more real.

MeMe Is Back!

On page 25, you read part of a draft about MeMe. Here is another way the writer might have written a part of that draft. Look at how the writer describes MeMe in this draft.

My imaginary friend's name is MeMe.

looks MeMe is two years old. She is half cat and half horse and has two wings. The cat half is red, and the horse half is white. **does** The wings are blue. MeMe likes to take me to and from school. We fly fast. One **feels** day, MeMe's wings fell off. MeMe needed to find a way to fix them. MeMe was sad. She asked me to help.

Time to Write

Look at a story you are writing. Then look at the checklist below. Ask yourself each question. Add details to your story so that you can answer yes to each question.

TFK Tips for Writers

Use paragraphs to organize your writing. All the sentences in a paragraph are about one main idea.

Checklist for a Story

- ☐ Did I give my story a title?
- ☐ Did I tell where and when my story takes place?
- ☐ Did I tell how the characters look and act? Did I tell what the characters do or like to do?
- ☐ Did I include a problem for my characters to solve?
- ☐ Did I tell how the character or characters solved the problem?
- ☐ Did I tell the story events in order?

What Is Nonfiction?

Nonfiction is a kind of writing that tells about real people and real events. Narrative nonfiction includes true stories about you, or personal narratives. It also includes true stories about other people, or biographies. News stories, reports, and reviews are also nonfiction.

Personal Narrative

A **personal narrative** tells a story about something that happened to you. Read this paragraph from a personal narrative.

A Day at the Toy Store

Mom picked me up after school. She smiled and said, "We're having Bring Your Son to Work Day at the store next Friday. Would you like to come?" Would I? You bet! Mom works in a big toy store.

TFK Tips for Writers

When you write, write in a way that sounds like you. Let readers hear what you are like and how you feel. **In other words, let them hear your voice!**

Written Report

A **report** gives facts about a topic. Writers find facts in different books and resources. They use these to write their report. Writers may also include charts, graphs, maps, diagrams, and photographs to help readers better understand their report. Look at the example below from a report about rabbits.

> A rabbit's sharp senses help keep it safe from harm. Its long ears perk up at the faintest sound. A rabbit's eyes can see in all directions. This allows it to escape from hungry enemies. Even its twitching nose can sense when danger is near.

TFK Tips for Nonfiction Writers

- Write about real people, real animals, and real events.
- Check your facts.
- Use photographs, charts, or other visuals.

Time to Write

Look at a personal narrative, report, or other piece of nonfiction that you are writing. Which tip could you try?

Finding Information

Good writers locate information and check their facts before they write. They find information in resources such as dictionaries, encyclopedias, and nonfiction books. They may also use an atlas or the Internet. What resources do you know?

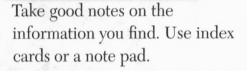

TFK Tips for Writers

Take good notes on the information you find. Use index cards or a note pad.

Encyclopedia Britannica Online

Sunflower
-looks like giant daisy
-name comes from way its head
  turns to follow sun
-food for birds and people
-used in soaps, paints, and chicken feed

 Find the smartest sites on the Internet at www.timeforkids.com/hh/rapidresearch

Identifying Main Ideas
and Supporting Details

When you write a report, each paragraph should have a **main idea.** Write a **topic sentence** for each paragraph that tells the main idea. Then add sentences with **supporting details** that tell more about the main idea. Read the paragraph below from a report on the Red Cross. Notice its order, or organization.

The Red Cross is a group that helps people in times of trouble. Helpers ← Topic sentence

rushed to bring food and water to people in Southeast Asia. Huge waves called tsunami caused floods in several countries there. The Red Cross sent ← Supporting detail sentences

tents, because the water had destroyed the homes of many families. Workers delivered medicine to keep away

sickness. The Red Cross helps people around the world.

Fact or Opinion?

When you write a report, it is important to present facts. You want to give your readers information that is correct.

What Are Facts?

Facts are bits of information that can be proved. You can prove a fact by looking, listening, or doing. You can also check in a trusted resource such as a good encyclopedia.

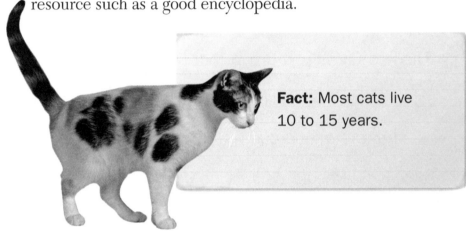

Fact: Most cats live 10 to 15 years.

What Are Opinions?

Opinions are beliefs that someone has. They tell how a person thinks or feels about certain topics. Words such as *I think, I feel, easy, good,* and *worst* are often used to state opinions.

Opinion: I think cats make the best pets.

Try This!

Read each statement below. Write F if you think the statement is a fact. Write O if you think it is opinion. How could you check your answers?

Fact or Opinion?

_____ All spiders have eight legs.

_____ Orb weaver spiders make the best webs.

_____ I think bats are ugly.

_____ Bats sleep hanging upside down.

Time to Write

Look at a report or other piece of nonfiction that you are writing. Underline the facts. Check them in a resource you trust.

TFK Tips for Writers

Nonfiction writing such as reports and news stories should be based on facts. Check your facts before you write.

I think summer is fun. There are seven continents. Green is a pretty color. There are 365 days in a year.

Writing a News Story

A news story gives important facts about a person, place, object, event, or idea. A news story has a headline that tells what the story is about. News stories often explain or give new information, telling readers something that they do not yet know.

A reporter often plans a news story around the **5 Ws and H.** This way, the reporter will be able to give readers all the important facts. Ask yourself these questions when you write a news story.

Who?
What?

The 5 Ws and H of a News Story

- **WHO** or **WHAT** is the story about?

- **WHAT** happened?

- **WHERE** did the event take place?

- **WHEN** did the event take place?

- **HOW** did the event happen?

- **WHY** is this event important?

Try This!

Read this paragraph from the news story below. Phrases that tell **When** and **How** have been labeled. Write **Who, What, Where,** or **Why** in the other boxes.

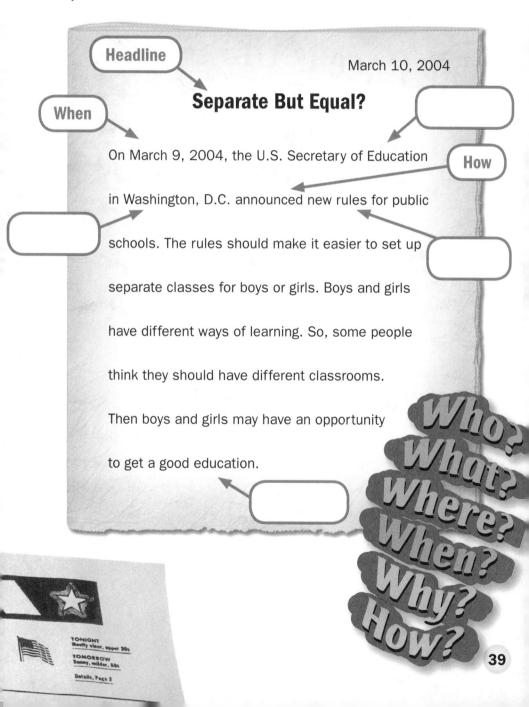

Headline

March 10, 2004

Separate But Equal?

When

How

On March 9, 2004, the U.S. Secretary of Education

in Washington, D.C. announced new rules for public

schools. The rules should make it easier to set up

separate classes for boys or girls. Boys and girls

have different ways of learning. So, some people

think they should have different classrooms.

Then boys and girls may have an opportunity

to get a good education.

Who?
What?
Where?
When?
Why?
How?

TONIGHT
Mostly clear, upper 30s

TOMORROW
Sunny, milder, 60s

Details, Page 2

Headlines

The title of a news story is called a **headline.** It gives a clue about the topic of the story. It should grab a reader's attention.

The Race is On!

Who Told a Secret?

Small Wonders

TFK Tips for Writers

When you write a news story, include a headline that gets your reader's attention.

Time to Write

Look at a news story that you are writing. Check to see that you've included a headline and the 5 Ws and H. Use the questions on page 38 to help you.

Writing a Biography

A **biography** tells the story of someone's life or about an important event in that person's life. When you write a biography, use the 5 Ws and H to help you organize your writing.

The 5 Ws and H of a Biography

- WHO is the biography about?
- WHAT did the person do?
- WHERE did the person do it?
- WHEN did the person do it?
- HOW did the person do it?
- WHY is the person important?

TFK Tips for Writers

- Choose just one event to write about.
- Use words such as **he, she, his,** and **hers.**
- Use past tense verbs if the person lived long ago.

Research Your Topic

When you write a biography, begin by gathering information about your subject. Encyclopedias, nonfiction books, and the Internet are sources you might use. If the person is still living, you may want to conduct an interview.

The following paragraph is about Harriet Tubman. It describes a cause that was very important to her—helping slaves gain freedom. Notice how the writer has organized the information to tell Harriet's story.

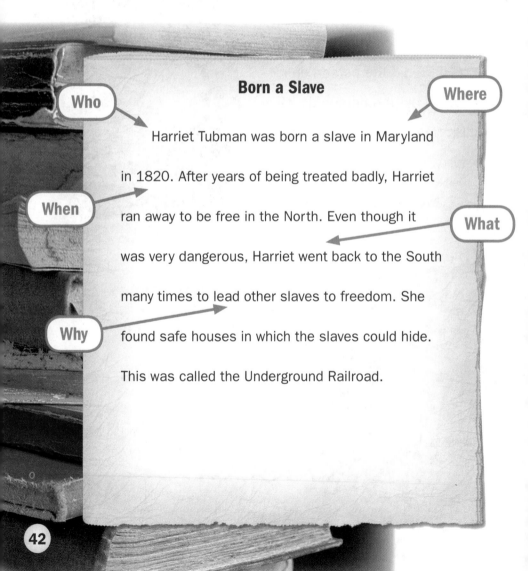

Born a Slave

Who

Where

Harriet Tubman was born a slave in Maryland

in 1820. After years of being treated badly, Harriet

When

ran away to be free in the North. Even though it

What

was very dangerous, Harriet went back to the South

many times to lead other slaves to freedom. She

Why

found safe houses in which the slaves could hide.

This was called the Underground Railroad.

Try This!

The paragraph below is from a biography of Thomas Edison. Read it. Which of the 5W and H questions are answered in this paragraph? Which do you think will be answered in the rest of the biography?

Chapter 1

Let There Be Light

It was New Year's Eve, 1879.

An inventor named Thomas Alva Edison

was about to do something that had never

been done before. On that December

night, he was going to introduce the world

to a new kind of light.

Time to Write

Look at a biography you are writing. Did you include the 5 Ws and H?

 Check out biography topics at
www.timeforkids.com/biographies

Writing to Persuade

When you write to **persuade,** your purpose is to get someone else to think or act a certain way. Depending on your audience, you might write a letter, a speech, or a review.

Start by choosing a topic you really care about. State your opinion or tell readers what you want them to do. Give reasons why you think that way. Be sure to include facts and examples that support your reasons. At the end, state what you want others to do and summarize the reasons why.

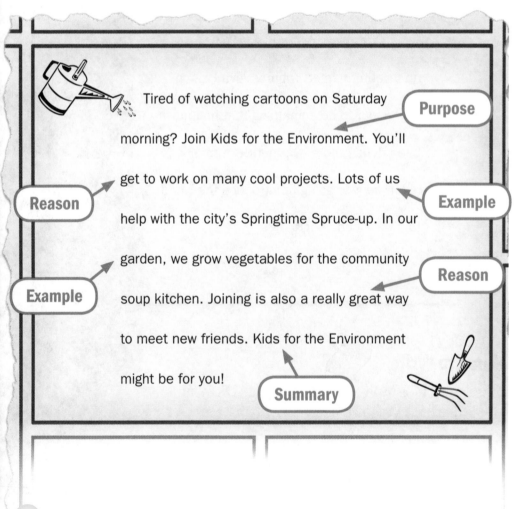

Tired of watching cartoons on Saturday morning? Join Kids for the Environment. You'll get to work on many cool projects. Lots of us help with the city's Springtime Spruce-up. In our garden, we grow vegetables for the community soup kitchen. Joining is also a really great way to meet new friends. Kids for the Environment might be for you!

Purpose

Example

Reason

Reason

Example

Summary

Strong Reasons

Good writers support their opinions with strong reasons. Compare the weak and strong reasons below. Why are the strong reasons better than the weak ones?

OPINION: Kids should not wear hats in school.	
WEAK REASONS	STRONG REASONS
• Hats look silly. • Hats are ugly.	• Hats block other people's view. • Kids play with their hats and make trouble in class.

Try This!

What is your opinion about students wearing in-line skates in school? Write it below. Then write two reasons to support your opinion.

OPINION: _____

REASON 1: _____

REASON 2: _____

TFK Tips for Writers

Write with a positive voice. Tell how taking a certain action will bring good results.

Facts and Examples

Read the letter below. What does the writer think people should do? Find one fact and one example the writer uses to support her opinion. What is the suggestion the writer makes?

Dear Editor,

I think that the town council should make a law to keep dogs out of parks. Dogs bark and chase people. Yesterday, a big dog almost bit me. Keep dogs out of the parks!

Emily James

Try This!

Now it's your turn. What is your opinion about dogs in the parks? Write it here. Then give one fact and one example you could use to support your opinion. Finally, suggest what the reader should do.

OPINION: _____

FACT: _____

EXAMPLE: _____

SUGGESTION: _____

TFK Tips for Writers

- Choose a topic you care about.
- Make sure you have enough reasons to support your opinion about the topic.
- Include facts and examples to support your reasons.

Time to Write

Look at a letter, editorial, or review that you are writing. Then look at the checklist below. Ask yourself each question on the list.

> Our town should have a doggy park. Dogs need a place to run and play.

Checklist for Writing to Persuade

- ☐ Did I state my purpose clearly?
- ☐ Did I include at least two strong reasons to support my opinion?
- ☐ Did I include facts and details that explain each reason?
- ☐ Did I make clear what I would like the reader to do?

Strong Openings and Closings

Strong Openings

When you write about an opinion, begin with a **strong opening** sentence or paragraph. A strong opening gives a hint about what your topic will be. The opening should get your audience interested right away.

Weak Opening

I like to play video games. There are many reasons I like to play them.

Strong Opening

I race to the computer. I pick up the control and hold it tightly in my hand. CLICK, CLICK. The adventure begins.

Try This!

Why is the strong opening better than the weak opening? Which words got your attention?

Strong Closings

When you write about an opinion, end with a **strong closing**. A strong closing sums up the important points.

Weak Closing

Now I've told you why I like video games.

Strong Closing

I like to play video games because they make me think and keep me alert. They also help my eyes and hands work together better.

Try This!

Why is the strong closing better than the weak closing? What are the writer's important points?

Time to Write

Look at an opinion you are writing about. Look at your opening. Is each weak or strong? Look at your closing. Does it sum up your main points?

A poem is a special kind of writing. A poem is like a song—it has *rhythm.* Some poems rhyme, and some repeat sounds. Other poems make comparisons. Still others follow a pattern.

These are all tools you can use when you want to write a poem.

> See, see! What shall I see?
> A horse's head
> Where its tail should be!

Play with Sounds

You can use "sound words" to add special effects to your poems. You can also add rhyme.

SLURP!
A sip from a drink that is cool.

SPLASH!
A belly-flop in my pool.

AHHHH!
Summer and there is no school!

sound word

words that rhyme

Time to Write

Write a sound word for

1 rain on a metal roof

_____

2 wind on a stormy night

_____

3 footsteps on the stairs

_____

Say That Again!

Repeating sounds will make any poem more interesting. Try saying this poem out loud—fast!

Betty Botter bought some butter,
But she said, "The butter's bitter;"
But a bit of better butter
Will make my batter better.

Time to Write

Dashing dinosaurs danced during dinner.

How would you complete these tongue twisters?

1 Two t_____ t_____ traveled to t_____ .

2 Fran found f_____ f_____ for F_____ .

3 Write your own tongue twister for someone to say: _____

_____ .

Make Comparisons

In a poem, you can describe things you know in a new way by making comparisons.

A **simile** compares two things using **like** or **as.**

The sun shines like a new penny.
The sun feels as hot as fire.

A **metaphor** compares or describes two things **without** using the words like or as.

The snow was a white blanket covering the hills.

Try This!

Read each comparison below. Write S if it is a simile. Write M if it is a metaphor.

_____ The stars were sparkling diamonds in the sky.

_____ Tina was as happy as an ant at a picnic.

Word Poems

A word poem follows a letter pattern. Look at the poems below. What letter pattern do you see in each poem?

Stars

Specks of
Twinkling lights
Always there
Ready to brighten the
Sky each night.

Carla

Caring
Artist
Redhead
Lively
Active

Try This!

Write a word poem like those on this page. Use each letter in your name or another word to begin a line of your word poem. Write the title at the top.

_____

_____

_____

_____

_____

_____

_____

Revising

Time to make changes to improve your draft

Can I Make My Writing Better?

Good writers think about what they have written. They listen to how their writing sounds and try to make it better. Reading your writing aloud to a partner is often helpful. The listener can tell which parts he or she likes and explain why. Your partner might also point out a part that is not clear and give suggestions for making changes.

Write Smooth Sentences

Joining short, choppy sentences into one longer sentence can make your writing better.

First Draft	Carlos is a great friend! Carlos is kind. Carlos is friendly. Carlos is cheerful.
Revised	Carlos is a great friend! Carlos is kind, friendly, and cheerful.

Time to Revise

To help you revise what you have written, ask yourself these questions:

- Is my writing clear?

- Do my sentences make sense?

- Will my audience be interested?

TFK Tips for Writers

Include both long and short sentences to add interest to your writing.

Is the Title Interesting?

A good title sparks your readers' interest. It gives a hint about your topic and makes your audience want to read on.

Try This!

Read the titles below. What do you think each story is probably about? Which stories would you want to read? Think about why you would be interested.

My Most Terrible Day
Tracks in the Wild
Mama Rocks, Papa Sings
The Secret Path

Time to Revise

Look at something you are writing. Give it a title that tells about the main idea and creates interest for your readers. Warm up by writing a title for a story about each of the following topics.

1 your favorite sport _____

2 a pet kitten or puppy _____

3 a fun place you have visited _____

4 a great invention _____

Is the Beginning Strong?

Begin with a sentence that grabs your readers' attention. Starting with a question or a surprise will make your audience want to read more.

Weak Beginning	It snowed last night.
Strong Beginning	When I looked out the window, I knew that this would be a great day.

Write a Catchy Opening

Try these strong beginnings.

Begin with a question.	Have you ever wondered how snowflakes form?
Begin with a quotation.	"That's just about the weirdest thing I've ever seen!" Rick cried.
Begin with a description.	Three tiny balls of fur nuzzled against my cat Franny.

This sounds scary. I love scary stories.

This sounds interesting! I wonder what's going to happen next?

Wow! This guy went to the moon. I can't wait to read more about him!

Try This!

Rewrite these weak openings. Write strong sentences that will capture a reader's interest.

1 I heard a squeaking sound in the kitchen.

---

2 My dog can do tricks.

Great Beginnings in Books

Read the beginning of *Charlotte's Web*. What is happening? Does it make you want to read more? Why or why not?

> "Where's Papa going with that ax?" said Fern to her mother as they were setting the table for breakfast.
>
> "Out to the hog house," replied Mrs. Arable. "Some pigs were born last night."

Time to Revise

Look at something you are revising. Does it have a strong beginning that will make readers want to keep reading? How can you make your opening sentence better?

Are the Sentences in Order?

When you write, organize the ideas or events so your meaning is clear. Put sentences in an order that makes sense to readers.

Try This!

Read the sets of sentences below. Number them to show the beginning, middle, and end of the story. Then read the sentences in order to tell the story.

_____ "Let's take a look," Mrs. Morton said as she carefully examined Fluffy's leg. Gently she removed a thorn and bandaged the kitten's paw.

_____ I can tell that Fluffy's paw is better now. My kitten is just as frisky as ever.

_____ Mrs. Morton knows more about animals than just about anyone it town. When my kitten limped over to its bed and lay down, I knew just where we needed to go.

Time Order Words

One way to organize your writing is by using time order clues. Words such as *first, next, then,* and *finally* can help readers understand how events take place.

Try This!

Read the paragraph below. Find the sentence that is out of order and show where you would move it. Then add time order words to show the order in which the events happen.

Backyard Fun

Every spring, Dad and I plant a garden. _____ ,

small green sprouts pop out of the ground. _____ ,

we prepare the soil. _____ , we plant the seeds

in rows. _____ , we water the garden every day.

Soon we'll have peppers, carrots, and beans.

TFK Tips for Writers

When you revise, number your sentences to tell how the events happened. Move any sentences that are not in correct order.

Time to Revise

Read over something that you have written. Would your writing make more sense if you changed the order of some sentences? Are there places where adding time order words would make the meaning clearer?

Is the Meaning Clear?

Sometimes changing the order of words in a sentence can change the meaning. Read both sentences below. How does moving the word *after* change the meaning? Which sentence makes more sense?

The boys pitched their tent after they arrived at camp.

After the boys pitched their tent, they arrived at camp.

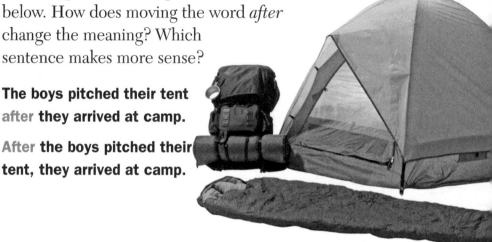

Try This!

Change the order of some words so the sentences make sense. Read the revised sentences.

1 Dad painted the lawn and mowed the fence.

2 Andy watched TV after he went to sleep.

Adding Details

Adding details will make your writing more interesting. Notice how details add meaning to the sentence below.

- The skaters glided.

- The **graceful** skaters glided **across the frozen lake**.

TFK Tips for Writers

Adding details to your sentences will help readers picture what is happening.

Did You Choose Strong Nouns?

Nouns are words that name persons, places, animals, and things. Good writers choose strong, **exact nouns** to make their writing clear and interesting. Look at the nouns in each sentence below. See how exact nouns give the reader more information.

First Draft	The **men** keep their **things** in the **building**.
Revised	The **firefighters** keep their **raincoats** and **helmets** in the **station house**.

Time to Revise

Replace the nouns in red type with strong nouns that will make the sentences more exact and interesting. Read aloud your revised sentences.

My class visited a **place** in the country. A **man** showed us fields where he grows **vegetables**. Then we went into a **building** and saw some **animals**.

Add to each list of exact nouns.

Persons

1. dentist

2. Grandma

3. _____

4. _____

Buildings

1. skyscraper

2. barn

3. _____

4. _____

Things or Animals

1. carrot

2. horse

3. _____

4. _____

Did You Use Vivid Verbs?

Verbs are words that tell the action in a sentence. When you write, choose **vivid verbs** that will help your reader picture exactly what is happening.

First Draft	The car **went** northward as hailstones **hit** off the hood. Maria and I looked back at the black sky. Maria **said**, "It's a tornado!"
Revised	The car **sped** northward as hailstones **bounced** off the hood. Maria and I looked back at the black sky. Maria **screamed**, "It's a tornado!"

Try This!

Study this list of vivid verbs. Then add interesting verbs that you might use in your writing.

Some Great Verbs

1 gazed   4 flashed

2 gripped   5 bounced

3 bumped

My Favorite Verbs

_____

_____

_____

Time to Revise

Replace the verbs in **red** type with more vivid verbs. Use words from the list above where you can. Read aloud the revised sentences.

I **looked** out the window. Just then, a bolt of lightning **came** near the plane. I **held** the arm of the seat and closed my eyes. The plane **landed** on the runway. What a ride that was!

Do You Need an Adjective?

Writers use **adjectives** to describe what they are writing about.

> **Adjectives** describe nouns. They tell how someone or something looks, feels, sounds, smells, and tastes.

spicy soup

noisy dog

picky eater

Try This!

Look at the sentences below. Notice the adjectives in red. How do they help you picture what the writer is writing about? Now reread the sentences without the words in red. Which group of sentences tells you more?

Liz received a **gorgeous** necklace as a gift. It sparkled with **enormous** blue beads. The color matched her **bright** blue eyes.

Time to Revise

Look at something you are writing. Add adjectives to make your writing more interesting. Warm up by adding adjectives to describe each item at the right.

1 _____ cat

2 _____ movie

3 _____ beach

4 _____ sky

5 _____ apple

Do You Need an Adverb?

Good writers use **adverbs** to tell more about something that happens in a story or other writing they do.

will finish
tomorrow
snored loudly
played outdoors

> **Adverbs** tell more about verbs. They tell how, when, or where an action takes place.

Try This!

Look at the sentences below. Notice the adverbs in red. How does each one tell about the action? Hint: Look for the verb.

Rick plays **inside** on rainy days. **Yesterday** he built a model racecar. He **quickly** glued the pieces together. **Then** he **carefully** painted the entire car.

Time to Revise

Look at something you have written. Add adverbs to make your writing more interesting. Warm up by adding adverbs to tell how, when, or where about each verb at the right.

1 spoke _____

2 skipped _____

3 answered _____

4 worked _____

5 sang _____

Editing and Proofreading

Time to find and fix any mistakes

Writing Great Sentences

Sentences are the building blocks for good writing. A **sentence** is a group of words that tells a complete thought.

Parts of a Sentence

A sentence has two main parts—a **subject part** and a **predicate part.** The **subject** tells whom or what the sentence is about. A subject has a noun. The **predicate** tells what the subject does or is. A predicate has a verb. Look at these examples. Name the noun in each subject and the verb in each predicate.

Subject	Predicate
Two boys	ran in the park.
Ellen	rode her bike.

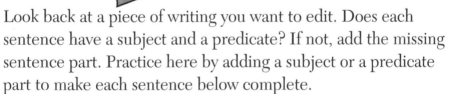

Time to Edit

Look back at a piece of writing you want to edit. Does each sentence have a subject and a predicate? If not, add the missing sentence part. Practice here by adding a subject or a predicate part to make each sentence below complete.

- A small brown squirrel _____

- _____ chased after a butterfly.

A Sentence for Every Reason

When you write, make sure you write the different kinds of sentences correctly. Knowing about each kind of sentence will help you do that.

Kinds of Sentences

- A sentence that tells something is a **statement.** It always ends with a period.

  My teacher is Ms Chavez.

- A sentence that asks something is a **question.** It always ends with a question mark.

  Who is Ms Chavez?

- A sentence that expresses strong feeling, such as surprise, fear, or excitement, is an **exclamation.** It ends with an exclamation point.

  You'll never guess what Ms Chavez saw!

- A sentence that asks or tells someone to do something is a **command.** It ends with a period.

  Tell me what Ms Chavez saw.

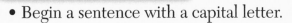

TFK Tips for Writers

- Begin a sentence with a capital letter.
- End a sentence with the correct punctuation mark.

Try This!

Add the correct punctuation mark to each sentence in the paragraph below.

Are you tired of puzzling over the answer to a

problem   Sleep on it   A study done in 2004

shows why a good night's sleep is important

German scientists found that people who sleep at least eight

hours a night are better at solving problems   Good night

TFK Tips for Writers

Read aloud the paragraph above. Listen to the way your voice changes when you read sentences with different kinds of punctuation.

Time to Edit

Read aloud a piece of writing that you are editing. Does the punctuation mark at the end of each sentence match the sound of your voice as you read?

Writing a Paragraph

Paragraphs organize your writing. A **paragraph** is a group of sentences linked together by a main idea.

Parts of a Paragraph

When you write a paragraph, include a **topic sentence** that tells the topic and main idea. Then add **detail sentences** that support the main idea. End with a **closing sentence** that makes your paragraph sound and feel complete.

Fun in the City

There are many things tourists can do in New York City. They can visit tall ← Topic sentence

buildings, such as the Empire State Building. They can stroll through the city's many different neighborhoods and parks. They can find food from around the world. ← Supporting detail sentences

Tourists will run out of time before they run out of things to do in this great city. ← Closing sentence

Try This!

Read the paragraph below. Then choose the topic sentence that best tells its main idea. Write the topic sentence on the lines at the beginning of the paragraph.

_____

_____

The burning sun rose higher over the city. People

leaned out of windows and fanned themselves.

Children sat limply on curbs.

Ice cream and cold drink

sellers were the only people

working. Even my dog

iPod was too hot to bark!

—— It was a beautiful day in January.

—— Nothing beats the excitement of city life!

—— How much longer could the heat wave last?

TFK Tips for Writers

Indent the first sentence of a paragraph. A paragraph indent tells your readers that you are beginning a new idea.

A Strong Finish

The closing sentence should make your paragraph sound and feel complete. Notice how the writer used a final sentence to summarize the paragraph below.

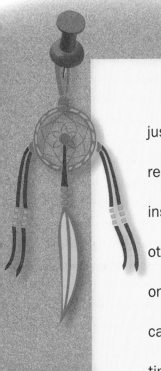

Children's museums today are not just filled with old objects to look at and read about. Children can play musical instruments at some museums. At others, they can build machines. Trying on clothes from other countries can carry children to a different place and time. Museums give kids of all ages a chance to imagine and explore.

← Closing sentence

TFK Tips for Writers

In a closing sentence, you can make a final comment, tell how you or someone else feels, or restate the main idea in a different way.

Using Capital Letters

Writers use capital letters to write proper nouns, the names of particular persons, places, or things. The chart below shows several other reasons why writers use capital letters.

for **names** of **people** and **places**	**Jim** and **Lisa** are my cousins from **California.**
for the **first word in a sentence**	**Two** polar bears played in the snow.
to write the pronoun *I*	Yesterday **I** played soccer with my friends.
to name **days of the week, months,** and **holidays**	**Thanksgiving Day** is always on the fourth **Thursday** in **November.**
for **important words in a title**	*Green Eggs and Ham* is a funny book.

Try This!

Read the sentences. Circle words that should begin with a capital letter.

1 My friend jeff lives in chicago.

2 we celebrate independence day in july.

3 greg read the book *half magic.*

4 Jason and i plan to go fishing in canada next august.

Choosing Punctuation

Writers use punctuation marks to show where a sentence ends. Look back at page 67 to review which punctuation marks to use for different kinds of sentences. The **comma** is another kind of punctuation. It tells a reader to pause briefly. Commas are used to separate words so that their meaning is clear. Here are some ways to use commas.

to separate three or more **words in a series**	Steve's favorite hobbies are drawing, reading, and playing baseball.
to separate the **month and day** from the **year**	My Uncle Frank got married in Chicago on June 28, 2003.
to separate the names of **a city and a state**	Last summer we spent our vacation in Orlando, Florida.

TFK Tips for Writers

Writers also use periods

- for **titles of people** written as abbreviations.
  Mr. and **Mrs.** Green visited **Dr.** Sharp.
  Note: The title **Ms** does not use a period.

- for **initials.**
  The letter was signed by Kathy **A.** Harris.

Time to Edit

Look at a paragraph, story, or report you have written. Check to be sure you have used capital letters and punctuation marks correctly.

Check Your Spelling

When you spell words correctly, others can easily read and understand what you write. Often it helps to compare a word you are trying to spell with other words that have the same sounds. Here are some patterns that will help you.

Sound and Letter Patterns

Long Vowel Sounds				
mail	he	wild	so	cue
play	deep	by	load	rule
take	speak	ride	note	
neighbor	funny	night	grow	

corn

night

Other Vowel Sounds				
fern	corn	mark	fear	how
firm	floor	heart	bear	round
word	pour		learn	
turn	board			

Try This!

Circle any words that are misspelled in the sentences below. Write the correct spelling above the word.

1 What did you lern from the book about bears?

2 As the stourm got closer, the wind started to bloa.

3 Jake fownd some shells on the beach.

More Sound and Letter Patterns

Beginning and Ending Consonant Blends				
trim	**sn**ap	**cl**ick	**fr**ee	be**st**

Words That Mean More Than One					
cat	bus	fox	dish	monk**ey**	penny
cat**s**	bus**es**	fox**es**	dish**es**	monk**eys**	penn**ies**

Words with *ed* and *ing* Endings			
jump	play	smil**e**	pat
jump**ed**	play**ed**	smil**ed**	pat**ted**
jump**ing**	play**ing**	smil**ing**	pat**ting**

Try This

Add an ending to make each word mean more than one.

class_____   box_____   hat_____   bush_____

Spell Syllables

Divide long words into syllables and sound out each part to help you spell the words correctly.

**wil•low   ti•ger   in•sect
im•por•tant   veg•e•ta•ble**

Time to Edit

Read something you have written. Pay close attention to spelling. Circle any words you are unsure of. Check their spellings in the dictionary.

Using Proofreading Marks

Proofreading is like detective work. Writers learn to look carefully to find and correct mistakes in their writing. All writers use a special set of marks to show what changes need to be made.

Common Proofreading Marks

≡	Make a capital letter	⊙	Add a period
/	Make a small letter	¶	Start a new paragraph
∧	Insert a letter or a word	℘	Take this out

Try This!

Look at the proofreading marks in the paragraph below. What changes would you make?

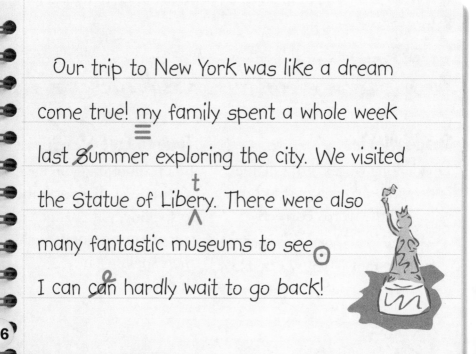

Our trip to New York was like a dream

come true! my family spent a whole week

last $\underset{\equiv}{S}$ummer exploring the city. We visited

the Statue of Lib$\overset{t}{\underset{\wedge}{e}}$ry. There were also

many fantastic museums to see$_{\odot}$

I can c$\overset{℘}{a}$n hardly wait to go back!

Tips for Proofreaders

Here are a few suggestions for finding and fixing mistakes in your writing.

> **Before you proofread, set your writing aside for a couple of hours.** You will be more likely to catch mistakes if you take a break and return to your writing later with a fresh mind.
>
> **Read aloud what you have written.** This is a great way to "hear" whether your writing makes sense.
>
> **Share your writing.** Have a partner, friend, or family member read your work. Ask them to comment on things they like and things you might do better.

Time to Edit

The following paragraph is the opening for a story called "A Super Bowl for Kids!" Proofread the paragraph. Use proofreading marks to show mistakes that need to be fixed.

Rain pours out of the florida sky like a waterfall. Mike Boyle is as wet as a sponge. Mike plays quarterback for the Huskies of Plymouth, New Hampshire The Huskies are playing in a final gme at the Pop Warner national championships.

Try This!

Proofread the passage carefully. Use proofreading marks to show the mistakes you find.

> On January 3, a spacecraft floo toward Mars at 12,000 miles per hour. Scientists at NASA had only one question: Would the craft land safely Then they got a a signal. "We see it!" cheered Wayne lee and others. The craft, called *Spirit,* had safely bounced onto mars.

Time to Edit

Proofread something you have written. Use the checklist to help you find and mark any mistakes you have made. Make changes and write a final copy.

Proofreader's Checklist

Here is a checklist you can use whenever you proofread.

- ☐ I wrote complete sentences.
- ☐ I indented all paragraphs.
- ☐ I used capital letters correctly.
- ☐ I checked my writing for errors in punctuation.
- ☐ I checked my writing for misspelled words.
- ☐ I made a neat final copy of my writing.

TFK Tips for Writers

Do you need to proofread even if you write with a computer? Yes! Computer spell-check programs catch some mistakes, but not all of them.

Publishing

Time to write your
final copy and share
it with others

Publishing Your Best

Good writers do not publish everything they write. They publish only their best writing. How do writers decide which piece or pieces are their best writing? Here are some questions you can ask to help you decide.

To Publish or Not to Publish

- Do I want to share this piece of writing with others? Why?

- Is my writing clear?

- Is my message clear?

- Does my piece of writing have a strong beginning and a strong ending?

- Is there any part I want to change before I publish it?

- Do I need pictures or graphs to make the presentation better?

TFK Tips for Writers

Publish writing that you like. Chances are that if you like a piece of writing, others will, too.

Ways to Publish Your Writing

The chart below shows a few different kinds of writing and different ways to publish them.

Kinds of Writing	Ways to Publish
Story such as a folktale, fairy tale, or adventure	• Add pictures to your story. • Make a Big Book. • Voice-record your story. • Put your story together with those of classmates to make a class book.
Personal narrative or biography	• Read aloud in an Author's Chair. • Dress up as the person you wrote about in your biography and tell your story to the class.
Report	• Make a booklet. • Add photos, maps, drawings, diagrams, or charts.
News story	• Make a poster to go with your report. • Put your news story with those of classmates to make a class newspaper or magazine.
Opinion essay, review, or editorial	• Post your news stories as part of a school online newspaper. • Make a comic strip. • Submit to a school or class newspaper. • Send as part of an email to friends or family.

Publishing on a Computer

You may decide to make your final copy and publish it on a computer. Use these tips to help you.

Create a Good Look

Design
Begin with a title page. Center the title and type your name below it. Then think about how you will arrange your writing on the rest of the pages. Include a mix of sentences and art to give your work a pleasing appearance.

Fonts
Using different fonts, or print styles, can add interest to your writing. Choose fonts that you like, but be sure they are easy to read. Italic and bold print are sometimes used to draw attention to special words or sentences. Here are some different fonts you might try.

Times

Times Italic

Helvetica

Helvetica Bold

Type Sizes
Choose a type size that makes your writing easy to read. A page filled with tiny print may be hard to read. Twelve-point type works well for most kinds of writing, such as stories and news reports. Use larger type and bold for titles and headlines. Compare these type sizes.

10-point type

12-point type

14-point type

Add Visuals

Art

Art adds interest to your writing. It can also help readers understand information you are presenting. There are different ways to include art with your writing.

- Use the computer's Paint or Draw features to create an original picture.

- Place computer clip art on the pages.

- Copy a photograph with a scanner. Then insert it electronically into the file.

- Leave space on the pages to draw or paste pictures after the pages have been printed.

Tables and Charts

Tables and charts give readers more information about your topic. They provide facts in a clear way that is easy to understand. For example, bar graphs can be useful for presenting the results of surveys and for showing facts about "how many."

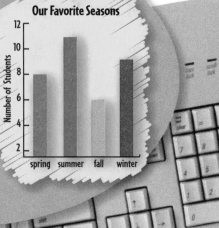

Our Favorite Seasons

Number of Students

spring summer fall winter

Print, Save, and File

Print

After you have made final corrections to your writing, print a final copy. You may choose paper with colors or special designs. Remember, though, that some colors can make your pages hard to read.

Save

You can save the file for each piece you have written on the computer in electronic folders. Saving files makes it easy for you to compare your writing with pieces you have written in the past. This will help you see the progress you are making.

File

You can organize your writing in separate folders. You might create a folder for each kind of writing, such as one for stories, one for reports, and so on. You might also make a folder for writing that you are still working on.

Sample Personal Narrative

The writer gives his or her narrative a title.

The writer describes an experience that happened to him or her.

The writer describes his or her feelings.

Keep an Eye on the Sky!

I was in gym class when my teacher suggested we go outside and play softball. As we made our way out to the field, my stomach slowly turned into a giant knot of fear.

Softball is just not my game. I have a knack for always getting hit in the head by the ball. It doesn't matter where I'm standing. The ball just seems to find me.

My teammates gave me a glove and put me way out in left field. I didn't complain. I just wanted to make sure I knew when gym class ended so I wouldn't be left behind.

The writer sets the scene and makes the reader want to know more.

The writer describes a problem he or she faced.

The writer describes the events in the order in which they happened.

The writer ends the story by sharing what he or she learned from this experience.

Nothing happened the first three innings. Well, things happened but not in my little part of the field. I started daydreaming. The next thing I knew, I heard the sound of a ball whizzing through the air. I put up my glove to protect my head, and an amazing thing happened. I caught the ball in my glove! Not only did I catch the ball, but I helped my team to win.

I was a hero to my classmates for the rest of the day. And I learned something. I may not always see the flying balls come my way, but I can always take a chance and try to catch one.

The writer gives details to help the reader form a picture of the events.

Sample Persuasive Essay

To Drill or Not to Drill?

The Arctic National Wildlife Refuge is home to caribou, moose, wolves, foxes, grizzlies, polar bears, and migratory birds. Leaders in the oil industry believe the refuge is the perfect site for the "environmentally sensitive exploration" of oil. Environmentalists are wondering: What will become of the wildlife?

President George W. Bush, oil-industry leaders, and others believe that Americans will benefit from the oil that lies under the snow-filled surface of the refuge. In their opinion, the oil will help reduce high fuel prices and decrease our need for oil from other countries.

The writer sets up the issue.

The writer includes a title in the form of a question.

The writer briefly states the different opinions on the topic.

The writer explains the opposing viewpoint.

The writer
explains his or
her opinion.

The writer ends
his or her paper
with an appeal
to the reader
to help solve the
problem.

I believe the cost of such drilling is too high. I agree with environmentalists who fear that drilling will disturb the migration of more than 130,000 caribou. Each spring, the caribou travel 400 miles to give birth on the coastal plain. In this area of the refuge, there are fewer predators. In addition, experts say that the oil in the area adds up to less than a six-month supply. Is such a small amount of oil worth the risk drilling poses to these animals?

Americans are the largest consumers of oil. Instead of drilling for oil, we should decrease our need for foreign oil by simply using less. We must all work together to cut back on the oil we use in order to preserve the wildlife of the Arctic National Wildlife Refuge.

The writer
provides facts
to support his
or her opinion.

The writer
provides a
suggestion
about how
to solve the
problem.

Sample Compare and Contrast Essay

The Senate and the House of Representatives

The government of the United States is made up of three branches: the legislative branch, the executive branch, and the judicial branch. The legislative branch, called Congress, is responsible for making laws. Congress is made up of two houses: the Senate and the House of Representatives. In this essay, you will learn the differences and similarities between these two houses of Congress.

There are many differences between the Senate and the House of Representatives. The Vice President of the United States is the head of the Senate. He must vote in the Senate if there is a tie. On the other hand, the House of Representatives' leader is called the Speaker of the House. The representatives elect him or her.

Another difference is that the Senate is made up of 100 senators, two from each state. The House of Representatives, however, is

---

The writer includes a title that lets the reader know the focus of the essay.

The writer lets the reader know what he or she will be writing about.

The writer provides a brief background on the two topics compared.

The writer uses contrast words.

The writer uses specific examples to show how the topics are different.

The writer uses specific examples to show how topics are similar.

made up of 435 representatives. The number of representatives from each state is determined by that state's population. The greater the population in a state, the more representatives that state will have in the House. A third difference is that senators are elected to six-year terms, while representatives are elected to serve two-year terms.

There are also similarities between the Senate and the House of Representatives. For example, both houses of Congress are made up of men and women. Both senators and representatives are members of Congress who must work together toward the same goal: to create, discuss, debate, and vote on bills, some of which eventually become laws. In the U.S. Capitol Building in Washington D.C., senators and representatives often meet with each other and in smaller groups to discuss laws. Before the President can sign a bill into law, it must first be approved by a majority of members in both the House and Senate.

Although Congress is made up of two types of lawmakers, they must work together for the benefit of all Americans.

The writer wraps-up by making a new point about the topic.

Sample Research Paper

Acid Rain, Killer Rain

Every time you turn on the television or take a ride in a car, you could be contributing to a problem called acid rain. In this essay, you'll learn how acid rain is created, the effects of acid rain, and more importantly, what we all can do to prevent it.

How is acid rain created?

Acid rain forms when the gases that are given off by burning fuels, such as coal and gasoline, mix with rain. Many power plants burn fuels in order to create the electricity that we use in our homes and offices every day. Cars and trucks also send these gases into the air when they burn gasoline. When rain mixes with these gases, harmful substances called acids form. This is acid rain.

The writer includes a catchy title.

The writer lets the reader know what the rest of the paper will be about.

The writer explains what acid rain, the topic, is.

The writer engages the reader with references to common activities.

The writer uses subheads to help organize the paper.

The writer states the main ideas in the form of questions.

What are the effects of acid rain?

Acid rain damages everything that it touches. It poisons our rivers, ponds, lakes, streams, and oceans along with all the life in them. It pollutes our soil and crops, weakens trees, and can even kill fish and plants. Acid rain also eats away at buildings and statues.

The writer shows the effects of acid rain.

How can we prevent acid rain?

We need to cut down on the pollution that gets into our air. Turn off lights, televisions, and other electrical appliances if you are not using them. Walk or take a bike whenever possible. If you are traveling a long distance, take a bus or train to save fuel.

As research shows, acid rain harms our environment. But people everywhere can take small steps now to help protect our environment for future generations.

The writer makes an important point to show what was learned from the research.

The writer suggests ways to prevent acid rain.

Sample How-To Article

Let the Sun Shine In!

Do you want to make a photograph using the sun? Then make a sun print! When objects are placed on sun-print paper, they block the rays of the sun and make a shadow. The light-sensitive paper records the shadow. Follow the directions below to learn how to make a sun print.

Here are the materials you will need:

- Light-sensitive paper (called sun-print paper) available at art supply stores
- Small objects such as leaves, shells, keys, and coins
- Bowl of water
- Sunlight

The writer tells the reader what process he or she will be explaining.

The writer lists any materials needed to do the activity.

The writer includes a title.

The writer explains what the reader will be able to do if he or she follows the directions.

The writer uses time-order words.

First, buy sun-print paper. Next, gather all the objects you want to use. Then, prepare a small bowl of cool water.

Take one piece of light-sensitive paper out of its pack. Notice that one side is blue, and one side is white. Be sure to keep the blue side facing down and out of the light until you are ready to use it.

The writer adds steps that will help the reader easily complete the activity.

Go outside. Place the light-sensitive paper on the ground with the blue side facing up. Place your objects on top of the paper. Work fast!

Leave the paper and objects out in the sun for two to four minutes. The entire paper will turn almost white when it is done.

Next, take the objects off the paper, and place the paper in the bowl of water. Soak the paper for about two minutes. The water stops the chemicals from reacting to the sunlight.

The writer also puts the steps in the order in which they need to be done.

Finally, take the paper out of the water and place it on a flat surface. As it dries, the paper will darken, and you will have a print made by the sun!

The writer explains the last step in the conclusion.

Homework Helper

Sample News Story

The title gives information about the story.

The writer tells the reader **what** this story is about.

The writer uses a quote from a scientist to show that he is important.

The writer uses a subhead to help organize the story.

A Double Dinosaur Discovery

Last December, two research teams working 2,000 miles apart in Antarctica made amazing discoveries. Each unearthed the fossilized remains of what is believed to be a new species of dinosaur. One is an herbivore, or plant eater, and the other is a carnivore, or meat eater.

Working separately, the teams led by scientists James Martin and William Hammer found the fossils. "There we were, in the middle of Antarctica, talking to Bill about his find 2,000 miles away," Martin told this reporter.

FROZEN IN TIME

Near Beardmore Glacier, Hammer's team found the bones of what they think is a plant-eating sauropod that lived 200

The writer shows **when** this event took place.

The writer's lead grabs the reader's attention.

The writer tells **who** made these discoveries and **how** scientists made them.

The writer describes what the scientists found.

The writer ends the story by explaining what will happen to the dinosaur bones.

The writer shows **where** this event took place.

The writer explains <u>why</u> this discovery is important.

million years ago during the Jurassic Period. On the island off the Antarctica Peninsula, Martin and his team found the bones of a type of theropod, a group that includes the tyrannosaur.

Each discovery will give scientists a new glimpse into the age of the dinosaurs. Any fossil find in Antarctica is rare, because bones and other remains are frozen and buried under many layers of ice. "We know very little about life in Antarctica from this time period," said Martin.

Excavating fossils is just the beginning. The scientists will start a yearlong process to analyze the bits of teeth and bone. "It's a detective story," Martin says. "You take all these bits of evidence and reconstruct the past."

— From TIME For Kids, March 12, 2004

97

Sample Oral Report

Come Visit "the Big Apple"

New York City is a wonderful place to visit. In fact, everyone should visit this unique city at some point in his or her life! Even though there are more than eight million people here, don't worry. New Yorkers like tourists!

New York is a huge city made up of five boroughs: Manhattan, Brooklyn, Staten Island, the Bronx, and Queens. The subway system connects the boroughs and makes it easy to get around. It's open 24 hours a day and runs throughout the five boroughs.

The title shows what the oral report is about.

The writer tells the audience what his or her report is about.

The writer includes facts about the topic.

The writer adds interesting details that the audience might want to know.

There are many things tourists can do in New York City. Often, tourists spend a lot of time visiting Manhattan. They climb to the top of tall buildings, such as the Empire State Building and the Chrysler Building, to see the views of the city. From 100 stories above the ground, the people and the cars on the street look like ants moving in every direction. Many of the buildings are old, and each has a story to tell.

Tourists can explore the city's many different neighborhoods and parks. They can eat in restaurants that serve food from around the world. They can visit stores and buy anything from a postcard to a car.

New York City, also called "the Big Apple," is a city full of history and interesting people. Come for a visit, and see for yourself!

The writer includes information that will help the audience make a decision.

The writer gives examples to support the main idea of the report.

The writer ends his or her oral report by encouraging the audience to take action.

Sample Biography

Mae Jemison: Star Child

Have you ever dreamed of flying freely through outer space surrounded by a sea of stars? Mae Jemison fulfilled that dream. On September 12, 1992, aboard the spaceship *Endeavour*, she became the first African-American woman to blast into outer space. This wasn't the only time, however, that Jemison had reached for the stars and realized her dreams.

Jemison was born on October 17, 1956, in Decatur, Alabama, but she grew up in Chicago, Illinois. There weren't many African-American female role models while Jemison was growing up, but she didn't let that stop her

The introduction grabs the reader's attention with a question.

The writer provides information about Jemison's childhood.

The writer includes the name of the person he or she is writing about.

The writer lets the reader know who the biography is about.

from achieving her goals. She was especially interested in anthropology, archaeology, and astronomy. Luckily, her parents encouraged those interests. That encouragement drove her to excel. She graduated from high school at the age of 16! The she earned degrees in chemical engineering and African-American studies at Stanford University. Soon after, she graduated from Cornell University's medical school. No obstacle was too great for Jemison to overcome.

The writer uses Jemison's education as an example that shows how she worked hard to achieve her goals.

Jemison's accomplishments did not end there. In 1981, she joined NASA's space program in Houston, Texas. In 1988, however, Jemison realized her biggest dream: She finally became an astronaut! Just four years later, she was named Science Mission Specialist on the *Endeavour* flight.

The writer gives examples of Jemison's career path.

Today she encourages young people, especially women and girls, to study the sciences. Her life example teaches us to follow our dreams, no matter how great!

The writer's conclusion lets the reader know why Jemison is an important person to learn about.

Homework Helper

Sample Book Report

The Bad Beginning: A Terrible Tale

Do you enjoy happy endings? If so, *The Bad Beginning* by Lemony Snicket is a book you'll want to avoid. This is a story with a bad beginning, a bad middle, and a bad ending. Why would anyone want to read such a bad book? It's all in good fun!

The Bad Beginning is a story about the suffering of three orphaned siblings at the hands of their uncle, Count Olaf. Although Violet, Klaus, and Sunny are the inheritors of an enormous fortune, they can't claim the money until they are older. For now, they must live with Olaf and cook and clean for him and his terrible theater

The writer's title includes the name of the book he or she is reviewing.

The writer includes the title and author in the introduction.

The writer engages the reader with a question.

The writer provides a brief summary of the plot.

The writer includes details about a problem the characters face.

friends. Why would such a cruel character take in three orphans? He wants to steal their fortune, of course.

The writer states his or her opinion about the book.

I can't tell you how the story ends, but I can tell you what I enjoyed most about the book. Snicket makes his readers laugh and want to continue reading, even in the most terrible situations. For example, he constantly warns his reader to put down the book because nothing good could possibly come of the orphans' unfortunate situation. He writes: "It is my sad duty to write down these unpleasant tales, but there is nothing stopping you from putting this book down at once..." Of course, Snicket's warnings only made me even more curious to find out what would become of the siblings in the end.

The writer provides examples from the book to support his or her opinion.

The writer gives reasons to explain why he or she recommends the book.

Will Olaf's evil plot win out? Or will these three crafty kids outwit him? If you're not afraid of a little misery and a whole lot of mischief, then I recommend you read *The Bad Beginning* and find out for yourself.

The writer ends with an opinion recommending the book.

Sample Business Letter

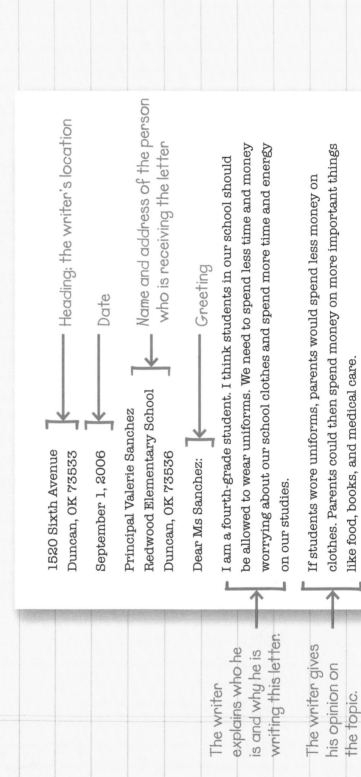

1520 Sixth Avenue
Duncan, OK 73533 — Heading; the writer's location

September 1, 2006 — Date

Principal Valerie Sanchez
Redwood Elementary School — Name and address of the person
Duncan, OK 73536 — who is receiving the letter

Dear Ms Sanchez: — Greeting

I am a fourth-grade student. I think students in our school should
be allowed to wear uniforms. We need to spend less time and money
worrying about our school clothes and spend more time and energy
on our studies.

The writer explains who he is and why he is writing this letter.

If students wore uniforms, parents would spend less money on
clothes. Parents could then spend money on more important things
like food, books, and medical care.

The writer gives his opinion on the topic.

If students wore uniforms, it would make it easier for them to get to
school on time. I spend a lot of time in the morning deciding what
clothes to wear. But if I wore a uniform, then I wouldn't waste time
thinking about clothes. I could focus on getting to school.

Students wouldn't worry so much about fitting in if they wore
uniforms. Kids are under a lot of pressure to wear the right clothes
and styles. Uniforms would show kids that it's more important to be
judged on who they are rather than on what they wear.

I really think this is an important issue. Students in our school
should be allowed to decide if they want to wear uniforms or not.

Thank you, Ms Sanchez, for reading my letter. I hope you will
consider my suggestion.

Sincerely, → Closing

Chip Woods → Signature

Chip Woods

Sample Poetry

The writer includes a clever title that tells what the poem is about.

The writer uses rhythm; read the poem aloud and clap along.

The writer uses internal rhymes within the lines (flop/plop; float/moat) to create interest.

How to Be a Frog

Don't stop, you frog, go hippity-hop!
Dive right in with a flop and a plop!

At the water's brim, dive in for a swim.
Beware the fish—you're dinner to him!

Here's the trick: Just do a frog kick.
Your webbed toes make you quick.

Then you'll streak without a squeak
Across any pond or river or creek.

And you can float like a log in a moat,
Or a smallish, greenish, tiny boat.

Underwater you're hidden from view.
Prying eyes can't see you.

But a fly you spy as he buzzes by,
And out flicks your tongue in one quick try!

Oh, froggy dear, your proud croak don't inhibit,
Sound out like a frog! Let it out! *Ribbit-ribbit!*

The writer creates a simile by using the word <u>like</u> to compare a floating frog to a log.

The writer made sure to rhyme the last word in each pair of lines.

The writer uses sound words.

Index

Traits of Good Writing Index